Th
It

o

(

THE
DOG
Artlist Collection

CARLTON
BOOKS

Introduction

We are mean, cruel, heartless people – but that's the way we had to be. It was like walking through a home for lost dogs with the adoring eyes of a thousand puppies pleading, "Pick me! Please pick me and take me home with you! I'll be good. I'll always love you. I don't eat much. Please pick me!" Then you turn your back and the little tail stops wagging, the sparkle goes out of the eyes, the head droops and a sad little bundle of disappointment curls up slowly in the corner of a lonely cage. Okay, maybe selecting the photographs for this book wasn't quite that tough, but with over 100,000 pictures to choose from there were an awful lot that didn't make it onto these pages!

The images were all specially created for "The Dog" using "strange ratio" photography, an irresistibly cute new craze from Japan that started as a series of postcards in 2000 and grew into an entire industry using doggy pictures on everything from t-shirts and bedspreads to back packs and mobile phone covers. What makes the pictures so appealing is the way in which the photography works – they actually manage to make it look as if you've just got the dog home, he's come bounding up to welcome you and stuck his face as close to yours as he can get, so that you can give him a great big hug.

As this is the very first time "The Dog" image collection has appeared in book form, we have tried to show as many of the most popular breeds as possible but while you sigh and coo and ooh and aah over the pictures, do spare a thought for all the sad little bundles that were left behind! ♪

This edition published in 2004 by
Carlton Books Ltd
A Division of the Carlton Publishing Group
20 Mortimer Street
London
W1T 3JW

A CIP catalogue for this book is available
from the British Library.

ISBN 1 84442 717 X

Project Editor: Amie McKee
Art Director: Clare Baggaley
Design: Stuart Smith
Production: Lisa Moore

Printed and bound in Dubai

# Contents

08 Golden Retriever

14 Scottish Terrier

16 Beagle

20 Rottweiler

22 Chihuahua

26 Newfoundland

28 Bull Terrier

32 Terriers

34 Shih-Tzu

38 Doberman

40 Shiba Inu

44 Japanese Spitz

46 Dalmatian

50 French Bulldog

56 Siberian Husky

58 Miniature Pinscher

62 Cardigan Welsh Corgi

64 Pembroke Welsh Corgi

66 West Highland White Terrier

72 English Cocker Spaniel

74 American Cocker Spaniel

78 Saint Bernard

80 German Shepherd

86 Old English Sheepdog

88 Basset Hound

92 Collie

94 Pug

98 Saluki

100 Cavalier King Charles Spaniel

106 Boxer

108 Yorkshire Terrier

112 Border Collie

116 Italian Greyhound

118 Chow Chow

122 Bloodhound

124 Jack Russell Terrier

130 Irish Setter

132 Dachshund

136 Weimaraner

138 Akita

142 Pekingese

144 Labrador Retriever

150 Maltese

154 Shetland Sheepdog

156 Bernese Mountain Dog

160 Pomeranian

162 English Bulldog

166 Boston Terrier

168 Poodle

174 Chinese Shar-Pei

176 Miniature Schnauzer

180 Afghan Hound

182 Papillon

186 Dandie Dinmont Terrier

188 Flat-Coated Retriever

Golden Retriever

Native to Britain, the Golden Retriever is one of
the top five most popular breeds in the UK. Bred
principally from yellow Flat-Coated Retrievers
(see page 188) and Tweed Water Spaniels in the
mid-nineteenth century, Golden Retrievers were,
of course, intended as gun dogs. Their dense,
waterproof coats and long legs make them ideal
for bounding into marshland or ponds to retrieve
downed game. Although the Golden Retriever is
a large and powerful dog, it can gently pick up
shot birds, hares or other game in its mouth
without damaging its quarry. Their gentle nature
has made them incredibly popular as family pets
as they are exceptionally good with children.

♪ *What's that smell? Is it you?*

♪ *People always give you a treat when you shake hands like this.*

09

♪ I teach the kids kindness, loyalty, patience and how to drink from the toilet.

♪ *Sometimes I wish I'd never joined this yoga class.*

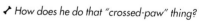

🦴 How does he do that "crossed-paw" thing?

Scottish Terrier

The Scottish Terrier is clearly one of the most distinctive of breeds with its elongated head, accentuated by the long hair that grows as "eyebrows" and "whiskers". Also commonly referred to as the Aberdeen Terrier or simply the "Scottie", this breed is short, stocky and strong. The Scottie was once used to root out badgers, foxes, rats and other pests, but is now most often kept as a companion. The Scottie's stubborn nature can make it awkward to train, but its loyalty is assured and it is an excellent watchdog.

♪ Look, here's my tongue to show
you where my mouth is ...

♪ ... now how about sticking a wee biscuit in there?

Beagle

Known as the smallest of the British scent hounds, the Beagle's ancestors probably came to England with William the Conqueror in 1066. Ideal for tracking hares or rabbits, they normally worked in packs. Smaller Beagles – called Pocket Beagles – were often carried in hunters' saddlebags and were kept as working dogs until the early twentieth century. The Beagle's coat is usually a combination of black, tan and white, and its white-tipped tail stands up as resolutely as its ears flop down. Alert and energetic, Beagles are remarkably affectionate and playful compared to some working breeds, making them fun to have around.

♪ Could somebody please help me with this stick?

♪ Hey, if I do this, can you see my lunch?

✦ *Alert and energetic, that's me.*

19

♪ *Is it tickle time yet?*

Rottweiler

The encumbrance of an undeserved reputation that has blackened its character – labelling it as ferociously aggressive – has not stopped the Rottweiler from becoming a very popular choice as a pet. In the 1990s, it became one of the top five most popular breeds in the USA. Generally calm and relaxed by nature, these strong and responsive dogs were originally bred in the nineteenth century in the town of Rottweil in southern Germany, where they were used for cattle herding and as guard and draught dogs. The Rottweiler's forebears were probably hunting dogs used for tackling wild boar – a formidable opponent that would have required a dog with every bit of the modern-day Rottweiler's strength and determination.

♪ *I know you didn't mean to burst her ball, but you'll have to apologize, otherwise she'll keep this up all day.*

♪ *Mexican? Really – can you see me in a sombrero?*

Chihuahua

The Chihuahua takes its name from the area of
Mexico in which it is thought to have originated.
The breed was first exported to the USA in the late
1800s, when the first few dozen Chihuahuas
caused a sensation among dog lovers – no one
had ever seen such a small, full-grown dog
before. Still regarded as the smallest breed of dog
in the world, the Chihuahua comes in a variety of
colours, with either a smooth or a long coat. The
latter was developed by breeding smooth-haired
Chihuahuas with Yorkshire Terriers (see page
108). Chihuahuas love human company, but need
careful handling as they are so small and frail.
They often shiver, not only when they are cold but
also when they are excited or nervous.

♪ And now a little song for old Mexico.

✦ *Those smooth-coated guys are wild!*

24

♪ *Hey! If we stand like this, we look like the world's only two-legged Chihuahuas!*

25

Newfoundland

The Newfoundland's powerful build, waterproof coat and webbed paws make it a very impressive swimmer – it is almost as much at home in the water as it is on dry land. It was as a general fisherman's friend that the Newfoundland was first known around 300 years ago in Canada, where it proved itself perfectly capable of coming to the rescue of fishermen who found themselves in trouble in the water. Although it may be descended from large breeds native to North America, it is thought that the Newfoundland is related to European mountain dogs that were taken to Canada by French fishermen.

♪ *Webbed paws? What am I, a dog or a duck?*

♪ I'm affectionate, see?

Bull Terrier

Also known as the English Bull Terrier, this breed was established – not surprisingly – in England. At the time, in the nineteenth century, dog fighting was a popular "sport" in England and the Bull Terrier was bred as a cross between the White English Terrier and the English Bulldog (see page 162) specifically to fight other dogs. Strong and courageous, Bull Terriers are now kept as pets, although they require careful training and do not generally get on well with other dogs or other pets. Despite the potential problems, however, Bull Terriers do make loyal and affectionate companions.

✔ *The best way to outwit a Great Dane is . . .*

✔ *... to hide underneath him.*

29

♪ She had beauty
treatment.

♪ I did! The manicure is great, but the facelift is a bit tight.

♪ *Bet you blink first.*

Airedale Terrier

Terriers

The Terrier Group of dogs come in all shapes and sizes, from the largest – the Airedale Terrier – to the smallest, such as the Norfolk Terrier. Very small Terriers like the Yorkshire Terrier (see page 108) or English Toy Terrier are classed in the "Toy" group, although they have the same sort of ancestry as their larger cousins. The name Terrier comes from *terrarri*, the name given by the Romans in the first century to the dogs they discovered in Britain burrowing in the ground after rodents, rabbits, badgers and foxes. *Terra* means "earth", and the burrowing instincts of the dogs the Romans called Earth Dogs still exist, as does their reluctance to back down from a fight – a throwback to the days when they faced up to their prey in tunnels with no option but to do battle.

Norwich Terrier

Norfolk Terrier

Manchester Terrier

Wire Fox Terrier

Welsh Terrier

33

Shih-Tzu

Remarkably similar to the Tibetan Lhasa Apso, the Chinese Shih-Tzu is one of the "Lion Dogs" of the Orient. The lion plays a major role in Buddhist mythology, having been kept as a pet by Buddha himself, and Lion Dogs are thus seen as having a link with Buddha. Developed in Beijing as a result of breeding Chinese and Tibetan types, the little Shih-Tzu has a long wavy coat. The hair around its face and head has been likened to a chrysanthemum flower, which is why the breed is also sometimes called the Chrysanthemum Dog.

♪ Mummy, he said we were
named after a sneeze.

♪ I didn't!

35

♪ *That's far enough! No more photographs!*

🦴 *No more pictures? But it took us ages to get the
whole litter together.*

Doberman

Collecting taxes was a tricky business in Germany in the nineteenth century. Not only were people reluctant to pay, but there were also plenty of vagabonds waiting to relieve the tax collector of his bounty when he was on his way back to the office. Ludwig Doberman came up with a solution to protect both himself and the tax money – he bred the world's finest guard dog. Doberman is thought to have crossed the German Shepherd and Pinscher (this guard dog is also known as the Doberman Pinscher) with the Rottweiler and Weimaraner before eventually coming up with the distinctive black-and-tan guard dog that is still used extensively by police forces and security companies more than a century later.

♪ *Hey, you! Have you paid your taxes?*

Shiba Inu

Looking somewhat like a smaller version of the
Akita (see page 138), the Shiba Inu – its name
means "small dog" in Japanese – comes from
the mountain regions of Japan, where dogs
of this type have been known for
centuries. The ancient breeds from
which the Shiba is descended have
existed in the mountains for up to
3,000 years, developing such
resistance to cold weather
conditions that the modern-day
Shiba is most definitely an outdoors
type. Also known as Brushwood Dogs,
Shibas have been used to hunt small game and
birds and have also participated, in the past, in
deer, boar and even bear hunting. Like so many
other hunting dogs, the Shibu is now kept more
as a pet and has become the most popular native
breed in Japan.

♪ *Hunt bears? Sure – we even look like bears ...*

♪ *... how about this for a bear roar?*

42

🦴 ... so they said I was just too silly for words and
   now neither of them are speaking to me ...

♪ *Hurry with photo ... can't hold ... head up ... much longer!*

Japanese Spitz

If you're looking for a colourful dog to keep as a pet, then the Japanese Spitz may not be the one for you. Like its larger Asian cousin, the Samoyed, from which it probably evolved in the nineteenth century, the Japanese Spitz comes in only one colour – pure white. If, on the other hand, you're wanting a glamorous companion, then look no further. The long white coat of the Japanese Spitz gives it the sort of movie-star looks that make this lively and quick-witted little dog a real eye-catcher.

♪ *We'd love to be a movie stars ...*

♪ *... we know we're not tall ...*

♪ *... but neither is Tom Cruise.*

Dalmatian

Although it takes its name from Dalmatia, a region of Croatia, the Dalmatian probably originated in northern India, from where it was brought to Dalmatia by traders. Dalmations were initially used as watchdogs, but by the time this elegant breed had spread further west, its good looks had turned it into something of a fashion accessory. In the eighteenth and nineteenth centuries, liver-and-white or black-and-white Dalmatians could be seen trotting alongside the carriages of their wealthy owners, ostensibly to ward off attacks by highwaymen, but also for show. Being fashionable also made the Dalmatian one of the most famous breeds in the world, when Cruella De Vil tried to turn 101 of them into a coat in the Disney movie *101 Dalmatians* and its sequels.

47

✔ *Did somebody mention Cruella De Vil?*

French Bulldog

If ever there was a dog with a colourful past it is the "Frenchie". These miniature Bulldogs were never actually used for the despicable sport of bull baiting but were bred from the smaller "runts" of English Bulldog litters by those who found the little dogs adorable. English lace makers are thought to have taken the dogs to France with them when they travelled there in search of work in the middle of the nineteenth century and the breed grew in popularity, becoming quite notorious when they were adopted as pets by Parisian "ladies of the night". Ooh la-la!

♪ *Unlike the English, we French Bulldogs have stylish ears.*

♪ *Bet you can't touch your nose with your tongue.*

♪ *Trying to stand? No, we're playing an invisible piano.*

Siberian Husky

With a wolf-like appearance that betrays its descent from the Arctic Wolf, the Siberian Husky was bred and kept as a sled dog by the nomadic Chukchi people of the eastern Siberian Arctic. In common with other northern breeds, the Siberian Husky has a double-layered coat, the inner layer providing insulation and the outer protecting it from the severe Arctic weather. Often confused with the Alaskan Malamute – though it is smaller – the Siberian Husky was brought to America and Canada in the nineteenth century by fur traders and gold prospectors who ventured into Asia. Some dogs in this energetic outdoors breed have amazing eyes of the brightest blue.

♪ *Blue or brown? I'm not telling.*

♪ *Okay, they're blue.*

Miniature Pinscher

Once used for hunting rats, the Miniature Pinscher can trace its roots back four centuries to native German terriers and is not, as is sometimes thought, a miniature Doberman. In a black-and-tan coat, the Miniature Pinscher can look very much like the English Toy Terrier and the larger Manchester Terrier, but it is far more distinctive in its red, blue-black or chocolate colourings. The breed was also known at one time as the Reh Pinscher, after the small roe deer (*Reh* in German) found in German forests.

✦ Owwwwwwww! I bit my tongue!

✦ He says he's very sorry to have done that in the house and he'll always go outside in future.

59

♪ *Thanks for sitting on my paws. It really warms them up.*

♪ *No problem. Going for a walk is tough when it's frosty.*

61

Cardigan Welsh Corgi

Although it's hard to believe when
you look at these little dogs – the
name Corgi is derived from the Welsh
words *corr* meaning dwarf and *ci*
meaning dog – their principle role as
working dogs was actually herding cattle!
Their short legs made them ideal for this task
as they could dart in beneath the cattle and snap
at their lower legs to get them moving, then dash
out of the way to avoid kicks. The Cardigan is
slightly larger than the Pembroke Welsh Corgi
(see page 64) and can be easily identified by its
long tail.

♪ *Spooky the way they stare, isn't it?*

Pembroke Welsh Corgi

Corgis are known to have existed in Wales for almost a thousand years. They are said to have been introduced by Flemish weavers who settled in the Welsh valleys in the early 1100s, although some believe the little dogs may have been in Wales far longer. Corgis could be related to Swedish Vallhunds and may have been brought to Wales by Viking raiders in the ninth century, or they may have arrived with Celtic travellers even earlier. Whatever their ancient history, the two different Corgi types are now firmly established as Welsh breeds. The Pembroke is the smaller of the two – the other being the Cardigan Welsh Corgi (see page 62) – has only a short tail by comparison, and is famous for enjoying royal patronage as the favourite pet of Queen Elizabeth II.

🦴 *We're small, but strong. See – ear press-ups.*

West Highland White Terrier

As its name suggests, the West Highland White Terrier is all-white in colour, except for its nose and eyes, and comes from the West Highlands of Scotland, where it was bred by Colonel Edward Malcolm of Poltalloch. Legend has it that Colonel Malcolm decided to breed only white terriers after his favourite dog, a reddish brown terrier, emerged from the heather during a hunt and was shot in mistake for a fox. Once widely used to hunt vermin, otters and foxes, the "Westie" achieved worldwide fame alongside the Scottish Terrier (or "Scottie", see page 14) when both were used to advertise a famous blend of Scotch whisky.

♪ I can bark the tune ...

♪ ... wag my tail in time
with the music ...

♪ ... and whistle the chorus of
"Flower of Scotland".

67

♪ But it's exhausting.

♪ Wow! They're cleaning the floor with a fluffy mop.

♪ *And it looks just like Uncle Angus!*

♪ *Get any closer to my tail and you'll regret it.*

♪ I hate being small …

♪ … can you make me look taller?

English Cocker Spaniel

Despite now being known as English Cocker
Spaniels – they were called simply Cocker
Spaniels until the American Cocker Spaniel (see
page 74) was recognized as a separate breed –
these dogs probably originated in Spain around
600 years ago. Their nationality is further
complicated by the fact that they were developed
as gun dogs in Wales, where they were used to
flush out and retrieve small game birds in the
nineteenth century.

♪ So am I English, Spanish or Welsh?

American Cocker Spaniel

The differences between the American and English Cockers (see page 72) first became apparent in the 1920s, although the American Cocker Spaniel was not recognized as a distinct breed until 1946. It has a much longer coat than its English cousin, and a longer neck, although overall it is slightly smaller in stature. American Cocker Spaniels, like their English relatives, are hugely popular as pets because they are very willing and easy to train, but their coats do require extensive grooming.

♪ *So's this!*

75

♪ *I love a good yawn. Apparently it's rude.*

♪ *When you're losing a race, standing on the other dog's ear is sometimes the only option.*

♪ *Ouch!*

77

Saint Bernard

The original and the most famous of all mountain rescue dogs is undoubtedly the Saint Bernard. Descended from a type of Mastiff introduced into Alpine regions by the Romans 2,000 years ago, the ancestors of the modern Saint Bernard were brought to a hospice in the mountains above the Saint Bernard pass in the Swiss Alps by travellers some time in the eleventh or twelfth century, although it wasn't until the eighteenth century that the Saint Bernard breed became recognized. Always intended as a watchdog, pathfinder and rescue dog, the Saint Bernard's powerful build and gentle nature made it the ideal guide for travellers lost on the snow-covered mountain tracks. Although thoroughly trustworthy and good-natured, the Saint Bernard's size, appetite and need for living and exercise space make it difficult to keep as a family pet, especially in towns.

♪ *Did anyone see these guys eat my lunch?*

♪ *Keep quiet if you know what's good for you!*

German Shepherd

One of the world's most famous and popular breeds, the German Shepherd only came into being a little over 100 years ago. A German enthusiast, fascinated with the intelligence, strength and agility of the country's native sheep dogs, established the breed, which spread throughout the world when Allied soldiers saw how the Germans used them as messenger, tracker and guard dogs during World War I. After the war, the name German Shepherd Dog (*Deutsher Shaferhund*) was dropped in favour of the Alsatian Wolf Dog (after the Alsace-Lorraine German/French border region), as it was thought that the word "German" would make the breed unpopular, and Alsatian continued to be used for the breed until the 1970s.

♪ *At last – a perfect pose and ... Oh, no! That ear's popped up again!*

81

♪ Just a few pictures? Okay – and you promise you won't make us look silly?

83

♪ I am not speaking to you.

♪ Oh come on! My dinner, your dinner, they all look the same to me!

85

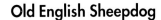

Old English Sheepdog

How on earth a full-grown Old English Sheepdog
manages to see where it's going from behind the
fringe of its long, shaggy coat is a marvel, but it's
that amazing coat that has made the breed so
internationally popular. The breed is descended
from European herding dogs, whose job it was to
protect livestock from predators as well as to
round them up, and the thick coat would originally
have provided protection not only from the
weather but also from attack by such predators.
For a large dog, the mature Old English
Sheepdog has comparatively small ears, which
are hidden beneath its long coat. It's tail (also
hidden) was docked quite short, resulting in the
breed sometimes being called the "Bobtail".

♪ *Cute poses guys. Now try this – the irresistible smile …*

Basset Hound

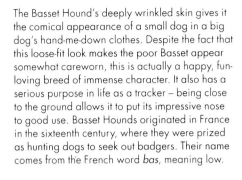

The Basset Hound's deeply wrinkled skin gives it the comical appearance of a small dog in a big dog's hand-me-down clothes. Despite the fact that this loose-fit look makes the poor Basset appear somewhat careworn, this is actually a happy, fun-loving breed of immense character. It also has a serious purpose in life as a tracker – being close to the ground allows it to put its impressive nose to good use. Basset Hounds originated in France in the sixteenth century, where they were prized as hunting dogs to seek out badgers. Their name comes from the French word *bas*, meaning low.

♪ *I'm a happy, fun-loving dog, just like it says.*

♪ *Are you saying that pie you left on the kitchen table wasn't for us?*

♪ *Why did you take that lovely old sock away from me?*

Rough Collie

One of the most famous dog breeds in the world, thanks to the Hollywood movies featuring the canine screen star "Lassie", the Rough Collie has a spectacular coat. Its slim face is framed by an impressive mane of hair and a proud chest frill. As well as being a movie star, the breed has enjoyed royal patronage: Queen Victoria kept Rough Collies at Balmoral Castle in Scotland. Although now mainly kept as pets, the Rough Collie's ancestors were used for herding sheep in Scotland, as were those of its cousin, the Smooth Collie, which shares its size and colouring with the Rough Collie but lacks that glamorous Hollywood fur coat.

♪ *Glamorous – that's me.*

🦴 *Go on, have a look at that fantastic chest frill.*

Pug

If the Pug's deeply lined, frowning expression makes it look somewhat elderly and a bit worried, then that may reflect something of the breed's lengthy history. The modern-day Pug can trace its family tree back more than 2,000 years to ancient China, although it did not arrive in Europe until around 400 years ago, when Dutch traders brought a few dogs home with them. Pugs came to Britain with William of Orange when he took the British throne in 1689 and they soon established themselves as a favourite pet of the aristocracy. Maybe today's Pugs are frowning with the perpetual worry of how on earth they will ever find their way home to China!

95

♪ Is this the way to China?

♪ And ... 1–2–3 ... 1–2–3 ... Darling, you waltz divinely.

♪ *See that backstroke leg action? And they still won't let us in the pool!*

Saluki

Also sometimes known as the Gazelle Hound, the Saluki, like the Afghan and the Greyhound, (see pages 180 and 116) has its origins as a hunter in the Middle East. The name Saluki probably comes from the Yemeni town of Saluk. For centuries Arab hunters used the Saluki to take gazelle – among the swiftest of antelopes – and held the dogs in such high esteem that to be offered one as a gift was seen to be a great honour. Although the modern Saluki comes in a huge variety of colours, it is nevertheless a most distinctive breed, tall and slim with a coat that is generally short and smooth except for its long ears and tail where the hair is long and silky.

99

♪ Yeah, but not now. I'm too sleepy.

♪ We used to catch gazelle?

Cavalier King Charles Spaniel

Small dogs kept as pets or companions and known as "Toy" dogs became extremely popular with European nobility in the sixteenth and seventeenth centuries. The King Charles Spaniel was the favourite of the English King Charles II, who used to walk his dogs in St James's Park in London. Over the years the breed developed a shorter, snub nose, but in the early twentieth century efforts were made to take the breed back to its royal roots, and in 1928 the longer nosed Cavalier King Charles developed. It was registered as a separate breed with the British Kennel Club in 1945.

🦴 *Take a look – any angle you like – us Cavaliers have got longer noses.*

101

♪ Zzzzzzzzzzzzzz ...

103

♪ Come on! Let's chase our tails!

♪ Shhhh! Don't wake the puppy.

♪ You know it's going to be a bad day when you wake up feeling like you've got two heads.

♪ *When I do this, the other paw is the longest. It's a worry, isn't it?*

Boxer

Fearless, strong and loyal, the Boxer is highly
respected as a guard dog and is used for police
work in some countries, although its adaptable
and responsive nature has also allowed it to take
on the role of guide dog. Descended from
Bullenbeisser Mastiffs and Bulldogs from Munich
in Germany around 150 years ago, the Boxer
was originally intended for bull baiting and boar
hunting. Despite its aggressive image, the Boxer
makes an excellent family pet. Its short, glossy,
fawn-and-white coat requires little grooming but
Boxers do need lots of exercise and attention.

♪ *Say you love me or I'll cry.*

♪ *We're tough, but we're soppy.*

107

Yorkshire Terrier

Now classed in the "Toy" group, the Yorkshire Terrier was once a working dog employed for one of the most arduous tasks any dog could undertake. The breed was developed by coal miners in the West Riding area of Yorkshire in England during the nineteenth century when they decided that they needed a small dog to take down into the mines with them to kill rats. The "Yorkie" that is so popular as a pet today is far prettier than the dog originally bred by the miners. Show dogs now have a long, silky coat of steel blue and tan that would be totally unsuitable to working down a mine, although Yorkshire Terrier puppies are born coal black!

♪ ... *so you promise we don't have to go down mines and fight rats any more?*

♪ *I washed my hair last night, now I just can't do a thing with it.*

Border Collie

Taking its name from the sheep-farming country on the border between Scotland and England, the highly intelligent Border Collie is renowned for its skill as a sheepdog. The extremely agile Border Collie loves to run, yet will remain perfectly motionless on command, intimidating sheep with a stern stare. Although known for their black-and-white markings, the breed appears in a variety of colours. The Border Collie displays great stamina: during the course of a working day it can run the equivalent of two marathons herding sheep.

✔ *The stern stare ... sheep hate this.*

♪ Yeah, that's scary!

♪ Stern? I prefer calm and confident.

113

♪ How about just cute?

♪ Run two marathons a day? Easy!

♪ Not if you're only little ...

114

Italian Greyhound

This miniature form of Greyhound shares its
ancestry with its cousins in what is known as the
"sight hound" group. For centuries these dogs
have worked with men as hunters – in the case
of the Greyhounds using their impressive
acceleration and sprinting ability to run down
and kill prey in open countryside. Similar hunting
dogs were introduced into Europe more than
2,500 years ago and have been found
mummified in the pyramid tombs of Pharaohs
and mentioned in manuscripts from Ancient
Persia. The little Italian Greyhound used to
be a hunter but now makes a quiet, gentle
and affectionate companion.

✔ *I smell dinner!*

♪ The mouth is watering ...

♪ The nose is twitching ...

♪ Nothing's quite as exciting
as a bowl full of food.

Chow Chow

Although not seen in Europe or the western world until the eighteenth century, and not firmly established here until more than a century later, the Chow Chow has long been a popular breed in China, where this powerfully built dog was prized for pulling carts and as a guard dog. In the harsh winters of Mongolia and Manchuria, its fur was also much sought after, as was its flesh. One feature of the Chow Chow, which it shares with the Shar-Pei (see page 174), is its unusual blue-black tongue.

♪ *Look at that – a blue-black tongue. Pretty unusual, huh?*

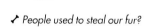

✔ People used to steal our fur?

✔ Don't even think about it! You'd look pretty stupid …

🦴 ... with a tail!

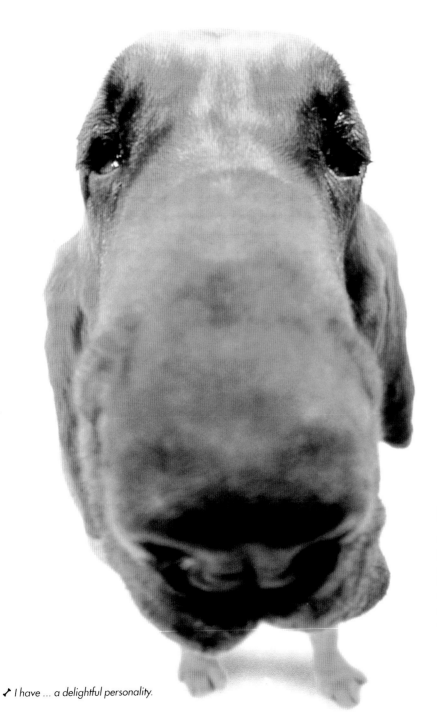

♪ *I have ... a delightful personality.*

Bloodhound

Without a doubt, the Bloodhound is the most famous tracking dog in the world. With a highly developed sense of smell, Bloodhounds have been known to pick up a trail up to two weeks old and follow a scent for over 130 miles (270km). Also known as the Hubert Hound, after the Abbey of St Hubert, where the dogs were first bred almost 1,500 years ago, the powerfully built Bloodhound was originally intended for hunting deer. Its loose folds of skin give the face a mournful expression, but the Bloodhound actually has a delightful personality.

123

♪ *Don't just stand there, fetch a vet – my chin's dropped off!*

Jack Russell Terrier

The Jack Russell Terrier, also known as the Parson Russell Terrier, takes its name from the flamboyant Reverend John Russell, nicknamed "The Hunting Parson", who bred his terriers for fox hunting in Devonshire, England, in the nineteenth century. The Jack Russell ran with the pack hounds but had the specific job of going to ground and flushing out the fox if it tried to take refuge underground. As a working dog, the Jack Russell has also been used for hunting smaller prey, notably rats. Predominantly white with tan or black and tan markings, the Jack Russell has become increasingly popular as a pet. The Reverend Russell would surely have been proud!

♪ So, you're saying we're all called Jack ... not just me?

🦴 *... then I gave the fox a left and a right ... like that ...and that ...*

127

🦴 *I guess everyone has one uncle who talks rubbish.*

♪ ...he also said he saw you licking the cat and he's ashamed to be your brother ...

Irish Setter

Also known as the Red Setter and originally red
and white in colouring, this is a fun-loving,
affectionate dog that will run for hours on end.
Although it now has a reputation for being
slightly eccentric, the Irish Setter was originally
bred, 300 years ago, with a serious purpose in
mind as a gun dog. It is ideal for bounding
through wet and boggy ground in Ireland to point
and retrieve game, a task for which it is still used,
although it requires more intensive training than
some other breeds.

♪ I know – let's go out and run for hours on end!

♪ What do you mean "We just did that"?

Dachshund

The Dachshund, sometimes affectionately known as the "sausage dog" because of its elongated shape, is generally thought to have originated in Germany. Dachshund, in fact, means "badger dog" in German and the breed was once used for flushing badgers out of their sets, the Dachshund's shape being ideally suited to scuttling down holes and along tunnels. Some believe, however, that the Dachshund may have a much older ancestry, as a similarly shaped hound has been seen in some Ancient Egyptian carvings. It was first brought to England by Queen Victoria's husband, Prince Albert, in the nineteenth century. The modern Dachshund stands even shorter than its Victorian forebears and has standard, miniature, short, wire and long-haired varieties in most colours.

♪ *Go on, shake a paw, any paw.*

134

♪ They call me a "sausage dog" but no one ever gives me any sausages.

So do I get a bone for this?

136

Weimaraner

The first Weimaraner dogs are believed by some to have been bred by the Grand Duke Karl August of Weimar in the nineteenth century. Certainly, dogs similar to today's Weimaraner were in evidence in the seventeenth century – Flemish artist Sir Anthony Van Dyck (court painter to British King Charles I) painted a portrait of Prince Ruprecht Van Der Pfalz in 1631 with what looks very like a Weimaraner at the Prince's side. Whatever its exact origins, the Weimaraner has enjoyed an unsurpassed reputation as an excellent all-round hunting dog, pointer and retriever for many years. Although there is a long-haired breed of Weimaraner, the dog is most commonly seen with a short, sleek, grey coat that has led to it being nicknamed the "Grey Ghost".

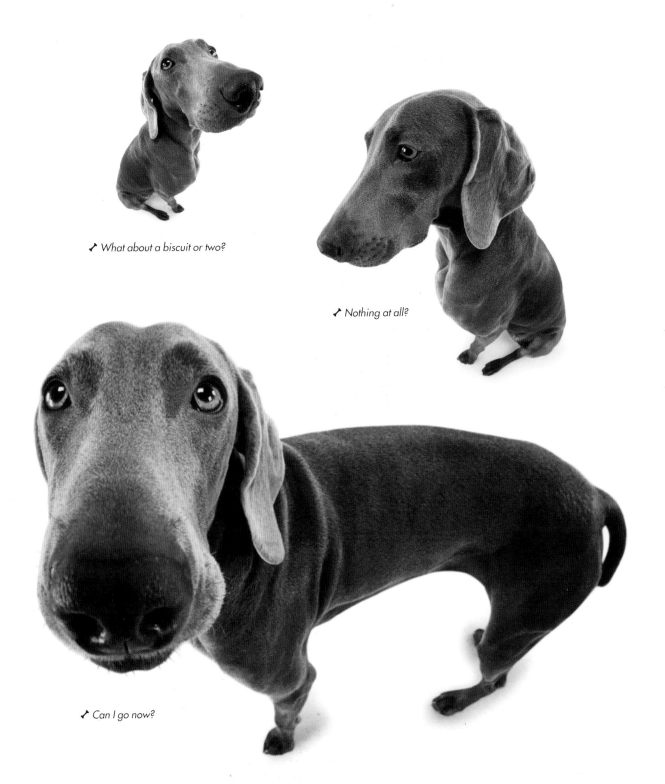

✦ What about a biscuit or two?

✦ Nothing at all?

✦ Can I go now?

♪ *Hey, did you know we were a national treasure?*

Akita

The pointed ears, narrow nose and curled tail of this large and powerful dog identify it as part of the spitz group, *spitz* meaning "sharp point" in German. Spitz dogs are among the oldest breeds known to man and were used to guard farms, encampments and travelling caravans as early as 800BC. The Akita, named after an area of northern Japan, was allegedly developed as a fighting dog by the Samurai, but was also used for hunting, guarding and herding. In 1931 the Japanese government honoured the breed by proclaiming it one of Japan's national treasures.

♪ Not me. Not since I wrecked the rug in the hall.

139

♪ Take the hint, won't you? Here's where the food bowl goes!

141

Pekingese

Of all the dogs that can claim an ancient royal heritage, the Pekingese has the most impressive ancestry of all. A favourite in the royal courts of the Chinese emperors for centuries, the Pekingese was also known as the "Lion Dog of Peking". Although small in stature, Lion Dogs were considered to be sacred and their theft was punishable by death. Their diminutive size earned them another nickname of "sleeve dogs", because they could easily be carried in the voluminous sleeves of courtiers' gowns. They were maintained almost exclusively as imperial pets until the British captured Beijing in 1860, whereupon some were taken to England and one was presented to Queen Victoria.

♪ *We will not be happy if you stick us up your sleeve!*

Labrador Retriever

Probably the most versatile working dog in the world, the Labrador is employed not only as a gun dog for retrieving wild fowl, but also as a sniffer dog with police forces and other emergency services, detecting drugs, explosives, contraband and even people. It used to help Newfoundland fisherman haul in their nets, a task that it also performed for English fishermen when it was first brought to Europe more than a century ago, and its friendliness and willing nature have made it a favourite as a guide dog for the blind. The Labrador Retriever is most popular of all, however, as a loving family pet.

✔ We are very loving ...

✔ ... and loyal and reliable ...

✔ . . so how about a treat?

✔

145

✔ *Look how straight I can get that tail.*

🦴 *Being a good friend is so exhausting.*

147

♪ *It's true! If you listen really hard you can hear the sea!*

Maltese

Once prized for its prowess as a rat catcher, the tiny Maltese was one of the first of the "Toy" breeds to be introduced into Europe, after which it became more of a ladies' companion and fashion accessory than a working dog. As its name suggests, it is generally accepted that the breed originated on the Mediterranean island of Malta, although it probably arrived there from North Africa around 2,000 years ago, and some argue that it actually came from Sicily. Whatever its ancestry, the modern-day Maltese is a lively, fun dog, good with children and a wonderful family pet, though its very long lemon-white coat does require extensive daily grooming.

🦴 Be honest – do I suit my ears in a bob like this?

♪ Check it out – pretty clean for a white dog, huh?

♪ Forward ... MARCH! Left, right, left, right ...

Shetland Sheepdog

The Shetland Sheepdog has the same attractive face and glamorous coat as the Rough Collie (see page 92), except that all those good looks come in a much smaller package. Just 60 per cent of the size of a Rough Collie, the Shetland nevertheless was a very effective working dog. It was bred in the eighteenth century in the Shetland Isles off the north coast of Scotland not only for herding sheep but also for controlling the native ponies and even chickens. Lively, intelligent and affectionate, the Shetland is small enough to tolerate life in town, making it an ideal family pet. Its suitability for domestic life has seen its popularity spread around the world, most notably to Japan – a far cry from its beginnings in Scotland's northern isles.

♪ *You lot handle the sheep and the ponies – I'll lick the chickens into shape!*

Bernese Mountain Dog

One of the gentle giants of the dog world, the
Bernese really is a mountain of a dog, tall and
immensely strong with a long, wavy coat.
Thought to have developed as a cross between
Swiss herding dogs and guard dogs brought
into the Alps by invading Roman soldiers, the
Bernese is still used as a working dog, although
not so much in its traditional role, in which its
great strength was put to use pulling carts of
farm produce to market. Although it is friendly
and enjoys life as a family pet, this hardy breed
is not best suited to living in towns, preferring
the great outdoors.

🦴 *If doing that gets him a tickle, I'm next.*

🦴 *Then me!*

🦴 *And me!*

158

♪ *Oh no! Tongue stuck to the floor again!*

♪ For my next impression ...
  the MGM lion – GRAAAA!!

Pomeranian

Originating in northern Germany and the Baltic region some 200 years ago, the Pomeranian is another small dog from the "Toy" group that has historically been a celebrity favourite. In the eighteenth century, the English artist Thomas Gainsborough painted his Pomeranian with her puppy; Mozart was very fond of his Pom and Queen Victoria had one that she called Beppo. Adored for their thick, fluffy coats, these sprightly little dogs have been bred down in size to become the smallest of the German spitz type – Gainsborough's pet would have been much bigger than the modern Pomeranian.

♪ *Now that's what I call a tongue!*

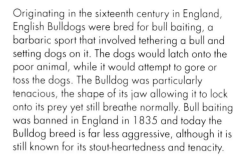

English Bulldog

Originating in the sixteenth century in England, English Bulldogs were bred for bull baiting, a barbaric sport that involved tethering a bull and setting dogs on it. The dogs would latch onto the poor animal, while it would attempt to gore or toss the dogs. The Bulldog was particularly tenacious, the shape of its jaw allowing it to lock onto its prey yet still breathe normally. Bull baiting was banned in England in 1835 and today the Bulldog breed is far less aggressive, although it is still known for its stout-heartedness and tenacity.

♪ *Have you got this in the same colour but a couple of sizes smaller?*

🦴 *Oooooooh ... it's that "too much lunch" feeling again ...*

♪ *One day my head will fit this face.*

Boston Terrier

Bred as a cross between the Pit Bull Terrier, the Bull Terrier, the Boxer and the English Bulldog in the Boston area of the USA around 200 years ago, the Boston Terrier was originally a fighting dog. Nowadays, the breed is sweet-natured and friendly, a far cry from its much more aggressive ancestors, which were generally used for killing rats. Boston Terriers are normally brindle and white or black and white, they have thin ears that look as though they have been borrowed from a bigger dog, and the Bulldog influence is obvious in the short, broad nose. An endearing expression betrays their fondness for human company.

♪ *Relax – I'm a lover not a fighter.*

♪ *Don't you just hate it when the wind catches your ears?*

Poodle

Descended from much larger French and German
hunting dogs more than 500 years ago, modern
Poodles are found in three different sizes: the
Standard Poodle, Miniature Poodle and Toy
Poodle. Their coats do not moult so they need to be
trimmed regularly. Although the remarkable "pom-
pom" trim is now purely for decoration or show,
working Poodles were originally clipped in this
way to keep their ankles warm and to trap air
around their chest, which helped them to stay dry
and warm when retrieving game from rivers or
lakes. The rest of the coat was clipped short to aid
mobility in the water. Poodles became the height of
fashion as pets in the 1950s, when the Miniature
Poodle became the world's most popular breed.

♪ *No wisecracks about feather-duster paws, okay?*

♪ *The good thing about our coats is that there's always a comfy bit to lie on.*

♪ *Ignore him. He thinks he's a kangaroo.*

171

♪ Life is such a rush! Breakfast-nap-walk-nap-snack-nap ...

Chinese Shar-Pei

Looking something like a Labrador in a Great Dane's coat, the Shar-Pei's most striking feature is its deeply wrinkled, loose skin. Although it looks rather funny and very endearing, the Shar-Pei's wrinkly skin has a sinister origin: the dogs were originally bred this way in China to make them difficult for other dogs to pin down during a dog fight. The Shar-Pei became known as the world's rarest breed and was on the brink of extinction when a Hong Kong enthusiast introduced them to the USA in the 1970s. American breeders have since begun a programme that has ensured the Shar-Pei's survival.

✯ *We were nearly extinct?*

✯ *No wonder we have so many worry lines!*

Miniature Schnauzer

As with the Poodle (see page 168), there are three different sizes of Schnauzer: small, medium and large. In the case of the Schnauzer, these are known as Miniature, Standard and Giant. Both Miniature and Giant Schnauzers have evolved from the Standard, which was crossed with larger German hunting dogs to create the Giant, used for herding cattle. The Miniature, which was used for hunting rats, is the result of a cross with smaller breeds. Like many other "ratters", the whiskery Miniature Schnauzer, also called the Zwergschnauzer, is classed as a Utility dog. Although small, the Miniature Schnauzer makes an excellent guard dog and family pet, but its coat – and especially those whiskers – needs regular trimming and daily grooming.

♪ I can't bear to watch. Who ever heard of a Schnauzer bungee jump?

177

♪ *You know how annoying it is when you get a hair in your mouth?*

Afghan Hound

The Afghan Hound is related to the Greyhound, a breed that developed around the Eastern Mediterranean many thousands of years ago. A powerful runner with excellent eyesight, the breed eventually spread to the Afghan mountains, where ruling princes adopted it as a royal hunting dog, using it to run down small deer or even wolves. The breed was introduced to Europe in the nineteenth century by soldiers returning from wars in the Afghan region. With its long, elegant head, slim frame and long, fine coat, the Afghan is an imposing sight, standing taller than a German Shepherd or a Doberman (see pages 80 and 38).

180

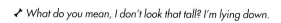

✔ *What do you mean, I don't look that tall? I'm lying down.*

181

Papillon

Featured in the paintings by artists such as
Rembrandt and Reubens, the little Papillon first
became a popular pet – especially with royalty
and the nobility – throughout Europe in the
seventeenth century. The name Papillon means
"butterfly" in French and reflects the shape of the
breed's ears, which stand proud from its head
like a butterfly's wings, as well as the white blaze
and symmetrical markings on its head, which
accentuate the image of a butterfly. The Papillon,
also known as the Continental Toy Spaniel, has a
very close relation called the Phalene (meaning
"moth" in French), whose ears hang down rather
than standing out like the Papillon's.

♪ Butterfly? Ridiculous! Ever see a butterfly with teeth like that?

♪ I don't see why I should be in trouble. I didn't rip up the newspaper.

♪ Well, it wasn't me.

185

♪ Or me.

♪ Or me. And what's more, nobody even saw me do it, either.

Dandie Dinmont Terrier

A lively, friendly little dog with a surprisingly deep bark that makes you think he must have a much bigger, ventriloquist friend close by. The Dandie Dinmont is a terrier from Scotland that may have evolved as a result of breeding native Scottish Skye and Skye Terriers with the German Dachshund (see pages 14 and132). Whatever its origins, it has been around for about 400 years and was used for hunting badgers, otters, foxes and rats long before Sir Walter Scott wrote his novel *Guy Mannering* in 1814. It was from a comical character in the book that the cheeky little Dandie Dinmont took his name.

♪ *If you must keep photographing me, can I please borrow a comb?*

Flat-Coated Retriever

These attractive and affectionate dogs were developed as working gun dogs in Britain and used extensively until the 1920s, when Labradors and Golden Retrievers started to become more popular. Although British, their ancestry lies on the other side of the Atlantic in North America, where they are believed to have been bred from the Labrador and the Newfoundland with a trace of Setter also in their bloodline. Black or liver in colour, the Flat-Coated Retriever is easy to train and, as you might expect from a retriever, it loves water and is an excellent swimmer.

🦴 *Ran five times around the garden ... exhausted ... need hugs ...*

✔ *He may like being different from the rest, but he's just as beautiful.*

♪ *Look into these eyes ... you love us ... you will give us biscuits ...*

192

♪ Help! Head ... stuck ... in ... hole!